MW01717607

BASIC TUMBLING

A Manual for Teaching Elementary through College Level

Donald F. Staffo, Ph.D.

american press

28 State Street #1100
Boston, Massachusetts
www.americanpresspublishers.com

ISBN 978-0-89641-444-0

Printed in the United States of America.

Acknowledgements

Thanks and appreciation to Andre' Bernal, Savannah Bernal, Megan Corthell, Hayley Elam, Brian McCoy, Ashlyn Perkins and Katelyn Perkins- elementary school students in the Tuscaloosa, Alabama City and County School Systems- for demonstrating the tumbling skills included in this book. Photography courtesy of Lucrecia Perkins, Luann Nix and Dr. Marilyn Staffo.

About the Author

Dr. Donald F. Staffo is a professor and chairman of the Department of Health and Physical Education at Stillman College in Tuscaloosa, Alabama. Prior to teaching at the college level for the past 27 years, where he has taught a tumbling skills class to physical education majors, Dr. Staffo taught elementary physical education, including an intensive unit on tumbling, for 10 years. He has also taught tumbling at the middle school and high school level. He earned his B.S. degree in health and physical education from the State University of New York at Brockport, M.A. from Western Kentucky University, and his Ph.D. from Ohio State University. He is the author of 7 books, more than 120 publications in professional journals, a weekly health and physical fitness newspaper column and over 1600 articles on physical education and sports in newsstand magazines.

PREFACE

Tumbling is a beneficial activity for elementary, middle, high school and college students because it contributes to many aspects of overall fitness, including strength, flexibility, coordination, balance and kinesthetic sense, and develops discipline, courage, self-confidence and self-esteem. However some physical education teachers may lack the knowledge, confidence and skill, and therefore may feel that they are not prepared to teach tumbling. Therefore, they do not include a tumbling unit in their curriculum, or may include a brief superficial tumbling activity simply to satisfy requirements.

In either case, students are deprived of a big-muscle activity that they might enjoy that would teach them new skills that would move them closer to reaching their full movement potential. Consequently, this book is for those presently teaching physical education or prospective physical education teachers elementary school through college level who want to learn how to teach a basic tumbling unit.

Basic tumbling and gymnastics skills can be taught *safely* so that students, including some who are initially afraid to tumble, are not only successful in learning the skills to varying degrees, *but also come to enjoy an activity that they otherwise did not believe that they could learn to like.*

For 40 years the author has taught the following basic tumbling unit at the elementary school through teaching physical education majors at the college level, with classes at both extremes including students who initially either could not do a simple forward roll or were afraid to even try. Utilizing the progressive and sequential methods and approach outlined in this book in a non-competitive, pressure-free environment, the result has been that most students either learned all the skills, most of the skills, or at least showed tremendous improvement, not only in skill attainment, *but in their attitude toward the activity.*

The underlying premises are that *if the skills are taught correctly, the students repetitiously practice the skills correctly* and are *allowed to learn at their own pace without pressure,* skill attainment will be dramatic. The more athletically inclined will rapidly advance to a relatively high level of skill in terms of performing the skill package that follows, with those less skilled or more timid gradually making significant improvement, considering their initial baseline skill level. Said another way, since people differ in strength, flexibility, agility, baseline skill and motivation to learn, everyone will not attain even the advanced beginner stage in tumbling. However, *if they adhere to what was stated at the beginning of this paragraph,* almost everyone should show improvement and attain a certain level of success. Therefore, an individual's improvement, attainment of skills, and effort to learn should be considered in evaluation, rather than comparing a less-skilled student to some standard of perfection or to someone with prior gymnastics training or natural ability.

Please keep in mind that people can be successful in this world without ever learning to do a forward roll or a headstand. But from an educational perspective, anytime someone learns to do something that they previously could not do, they are not only excited to a certain extent (elementary and college students alike all yell for the teacher to look when they successfully perform a skill for the first time), but also feel a little bit better about themselves. This little boost in self-esteem is very important, especially at the elementary school level, where many times children rightly or wrongly pick the people who they want to be their friends based on how well they play or perform physical skills. That is because play is a natural activity for children, and children tend to want to be friends with people who play well and skillfully.

Consequently, since tumbling is not something most young children learn routinely growing up the way many do basketball or baseball, tumbling provides a great opportunity for the physical educator to teach an activity that many children do not know how to do and some may initially fear. Therefore when students, or people of all ages for that matter, learn skills they previously never imagined they could do, their self-esteem is enhanced. With increased self-esteem and the added confidence that goes along with it, students are more apt to attempt other skills or try other activities that they cannot do and prior to this little bit of tumbling success may not otherwise have tried. It is a simple application of the old adage, "success breeds success." That is why, *if emphasis is placed in the proper places*, students regardless of skill attainment will usually come away with increased confidence and at the very least with a much better attitude toward tumbling.

This book is intended as a guide to help instructors safely teach tumbling fundamentals in a physical education setting, *not* for coaching a gymnastics team. Therefore the level of skill attainment included in the following skills package will at best be advanced beginner, which is sufficient for students at the novice tumbling level in a typical physical education class at the public school and college level.

It will be dependent on the philosophy, attitude, empathy and teaching methodology of the teacher whether the student(s) will leave more skilled and with not only enhanced self-esteem and a better attitude toward tumbling, or frustrated and with hatred toward what could and should be a beneficial big-muscle activity.

Contents

FOREWORD

Historically, gymnastics was very important in early Greek and German culture. Early Greek philosophy emphasized the body beautiful. With its ability to build a strong body, gymnastics became an integral part of the educational process. Gymnastics in the mid to late 1700s became popular in Germany, Czechoslovakia and other countries. In the early and mid-1800s Germans migrated to the U.S. and founded the German Turnvereins, or Turner Society, which had the motto of "a sound mind in a sound body." Dr. Charles Beck introduced the German system to America in 1825.

About the same time Czechoslovakians brought the "Sokol" gymnastics system of training to the U.S., with the Turners and the Sokols having a significant influence in the development of gymnastics in America. Soon joining them in the U.S. were Slavs, Swiss, Swedes and migrants from other countries, who came to America and brought with them their backgrounds in gymnastics. They started organizing their own gymnastics clubs, similar to the Turners and the Sokol systems. Gymnastics therefore became the basis for the early physical training and physical education programs in the U.S., with Americans Catherine Beecher and Dio Lewis the early leaders.

By the 1930s, however, gymnastics began to decline in the U.S. Due to televised coverage of the 1960 Olympic Games, gymnastics experienced a renewal of interest in this country.

In the Olympic Games that followed, medal winners such as Peter Korman, Bart Conner, Peter Vidmar, Cathy Rigby, Olga Korbut, Nadia Comanecei, Mary Lou Retton, Pheobe Mills and Shannon Miller increased the popularity of gymnastics in America.

Because of the benefits that can be derived from participation in this big-muscle activity- such as strength development, flexibility, agility, balance, coordination, discipline, self-confidence, courage and kinesthetic awareness- tumbling or basic gymnastics should be an integral part of the physical education program in the elementary school through college level. Basic tumbling or gymnastics challenges students at all levels and provides students opportunities to work by themselves or with small and large groups. A four-week unit in tumbling and basic gymnastics would accomplish a number of integral physical education objectives.

The reasons that tumbling and basic gymnastics are no longer a part of many physical education curriculums is because today many physical education teachers are not trained or confident to teach basic tumbling, and because since they never learned how to tumble, they have no interest in the activity. Therefore, unfortunately, they do not teach tumbling, with the students then losing an opportunity to learn something new and beneficial.

Contrary to popular belief, tumbling and gymnastics activity does not necessarily result in more injuries than other organized sports activities. As with other sports activities, *safety must be a primary concern.* Competent and responsible teaching can prevent unnecessary injuries.

This book is intended to provide instruction on how to correctly and safely teach basic tumbling skills and activities so that more physical educators will feel confident in including the unit in their school physical education curriculums. Although there are other teaching methods, for safety reasons the author prefers the command or direct style for teaching tumbling.

When physical educators see the success students have in tumbling and the enjoyment and excitement that students receive when they first perform a tumbling skill that they previously could not do, physical educators should readily see the benefits of teaching tumbling. Physical educators should also realize that when they omit tumbling from the curriculum they are short-changing their students and depriving them of this experience and the resultant satisfaction and self-esteem enhancement students can derive from tumbling.

Chapter 1

INTRODUCTION

General Objectives for a Tumbling Unit

For students to:

1. participate in a vigorous, big-muscle activity
2. develop a kinesthetic sense of general and specific body control
3. increase muscular strength and endurance
4. increase flexibility
5. improve coordination
6. learn to work by ones self, with a partner or in small or large group
7. develop a level of conditioning to participate fully in the activity
8. learn basic tumbling skills and simple partner and group stunts
9. to appreciate the activity of tumbling and the skill possessed by accomplished gymnasts

Specific Objectives for Physical Education Majors or Physical Educators

For physical education majors or physical educators to:

1. be able to demonstrate, or identify a student who can correctly demonstrate, the basic individual skills included in the skills package (a picture is worth a thousand words)
2. be able to identify the critical parts of each skill (task analysis)
3. understand correct teaching methodology for tumbling
4. be able to safely and correctly teach the fundamentals of tumbling
5. guide and inspire students to reach their highest movement potentials
6. be able to teach how to put tumbling moves together into a routine (stringing several moves together going from one maneuver into another)

Keep in Mind

1. *safety must be emphasized* first and foremost (it is the *responsibility of the teacher* to provide a safe environment); this includes clean and appropriate panelite or folding mats at least one inch thick, correct teaching, as well as teaching how, when and where to spot (please see below)
2. make sure students are properly warmed up with plenty of total body, head-to-toe bending and stretching prior to tumbling (10 minutes minimum); for flexibility full-stretch /static stretching should be done, with stretch positions held for at least a slow 10-second count
3. *skills must be taught progressively from easy to difficult*
4. teaching methodology should incorporate:
   - Explanation
   - Demonstration

- Allowance of time for students to practice skills
- Correction of mistakes (*task analysis)
- Evaluation

*(task analysis: before improvement can be made, the teacher must *recognize what the student is doing wrong* and *articulate how to correct it*)

5. teach students *how, when* and *where* to spot (physically assisting a student performing a skill, communicating what is being done correctly or incorrectly and/or being in position to prevent a student performing a skill from being injured), as spotting is the single most important safety factor in preventing injuries; protecting the tumbler must be the primary concern, with particular emphasis on preventing the tumbler's head from hitting the floor
6. be aware of negligence and liability issues
7. students should not tumble, practice, or play on the mats unsupervised
8. students should remove all jewelry before tumbling and have nothing in their mouths
9. understand individual differences and *allow students to progress at their own rate,* never letting any students attempt more advanced skills until they have mastered the fundamentals, lead-up or pre-requisite skills
10. students should practice in the same direction to avoid collisions or falling on each other
11. encourage students to rest periodically as fatigue increases chance of injury
12. understand that *if students are taught correctly, if they practice the skills correctly and repetitiously,* that sooner or later skill attainment or recognizable improvement will occur

13. keep the participants actively involved in on-task activity at all times; students should practice skills that do not require spotting by themselves, while waiting to work one-on-one with the teacher and/or spotters on more difficult skills

When Reading this Book

Please understand that many skills are pictured or described from either the left or right side or from a particular angle. Therefore such skills can also be performed from the opposite side by simply reversing arm or leg movement. Skills are listed in a suggested progressive order from easy to difficult, ***but as with everything in this book, teachers must use professional judgment, common sense and discretion in determining precisely how to best teach certain things based on their particular situation, background and level of expertise/experience.***

Class Organization

1. well-padded panelite mats at least one inch thick can be placed end to end across the gym or floor (more rows of mats with shorter lines of students will provide students with more on-task activity time and less waiting in line for their turn)
2. skills may be practiced across the length or width of the mat
3. consider age, maturity, skill level and number of students in class when determining how best to teach the tumbling unit
4. a simple pre-test can ascertain each student's baseline skill level

5. students may be organized into ability groups, or highly skilled students can be paired with lesser skilled students so the higher skilled students can assist the lesser skilled students
6. students with highest skill levels for particular maneuvers should be placed in the front of the line so other students can observe how the skill is done correctly before it is their turn to attempt the skill

Chapter 2

Basic Skills Package

Front Scale Position

Teaching Tips:

1. stand on one straight leg
2. extend other leg backward as high as possible without bending knees and keeping the foot stretched
3. head and upper body are out in front, with back slightly arched
4. arms can be held shoulder level and to the sides

Common Mistakes:

1. extended leg bent or not high enough
2. head and upper body not leaning forward enough
3. back not arched

Side Scale Position

Teaching Tips:

1. stand on one leg
2. extend other leg to the side
3. keep extended leg high and straight
4. lean body away from extended leg to maintain balance
5. extend and keep arms straight to side and slightly raised

Common Mistakes:

1. extended leg is not high enough
2. extended leg is bent
3. not enough lean to side opposite extended leg

L-Hold Balance

Teaching Tips:

1. sit on mat with legs forward, straight and together
2. with arms straight, push up and lift buttocks and legs off of the mat

Common Mistakes:

1. a problem if not strong enough to lift body off mat
2. legs are not held straight or together

Straddle Balance

Teaching Tips:

1. sit on mat with legs straight and in a V-position
2. hands on mat between legs
3. with straight arms, lift buttocks and legs off of the mat

Common Mistakes:

1. a problem if not strong enough to lift body off mat
2. legs are not held straight

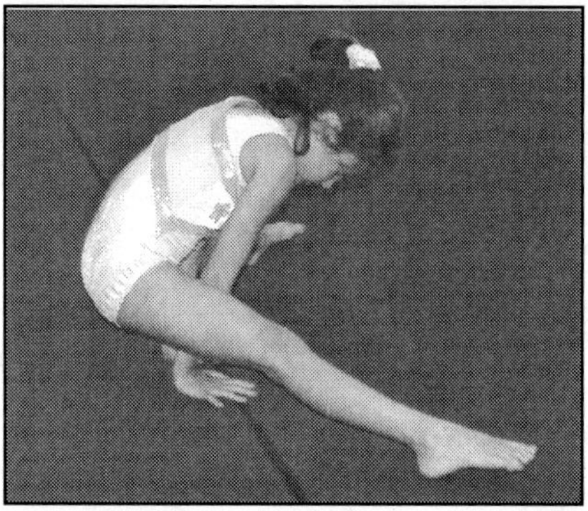

Swedish Fall

Teaching Tips:

1. start with a front scale position
2. drop forward smoothly onto hands, bending the elbows while keeping the back leg straight in the air
3. be careful to break fall with hands, lowering yourself without hitting chin or face on the mat

Common Mistake:

1. tendency to lower yourself instead of dropping

Tripod (3-point balance)

Teaching Tips:

1. start from a squat position on the mat
2. place hands on the floor shoulder width apart with fingers wide apart to provide a wide base for better support and balance
3. bend elbows and rest knees on elbows
4. slowly tip forward with knees still resting on elbows so forehead is on the mat in front of the hands
5. head and hands form a wide triangle base
6. balance in a tripod or 3-point balance with knees on elbows for 5 seconds

Common Mistakes:

1. hands placed too close together; fingers not spread apart
2. head not placed far enough in front to form point of triangle

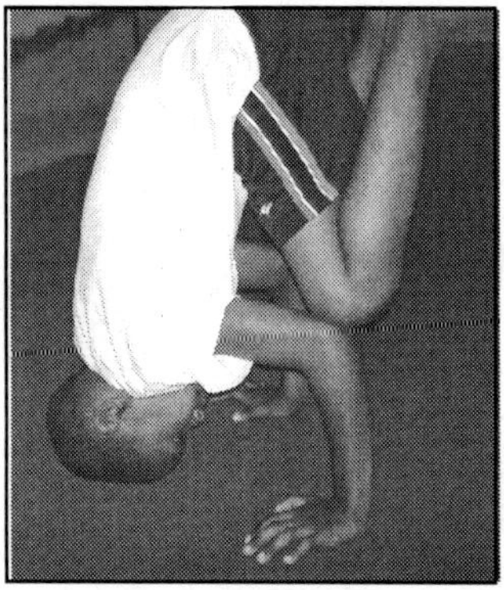

Headstand

Teaching Tips:

1. from a tripod and *without moving hands or head from triangle base,* slowly lift legs up straight (may need assistance from a spotter at first)
2. concentrate on arching back slightly and keeping legs straight and knees and feet together
3. point toes and stretch legs toward the ceiling
4. hold steady for a 5-count
5. beginners should come down the same way they went up, lowering legs to the mat; later *after they learn the forward roll,* they can learn to tuck their chin and roll out of the head stand

Common Mistakes:

1. not establishing a solid tripod base before lifting legs (draw triangles on the mat showing where hands and head should be placed)
2. moving hands to break the tripod base while lifting legs
3. not arching back so legs are not straight up (rear end sticks out)
4. not keeping legs straight (knees are bent) and together
5. allowing arms to wobble or collapse

Headstand From Prone Position

Teaching Tips:

1. lie on belly with arms out in front or to the side and palms on the mat, shoulder width apart and fingers wide apart (similar to tripod position above)
2. pull forward on mat until head is in front in tripod position while lifting hips and keeping legs straight; without moving hands or head from tripod base, slowly pull or drag legs forward
3. using stomach muscles and keeping legs straight, slowly lift legs toward ceiling and into a headstand
4. arch back, keep legs straight, knees together, point toes and stretch legs toward ceiling
5. beginners should come down the same way they went up, lowering legs to the mat (see teaching tips for headstand)

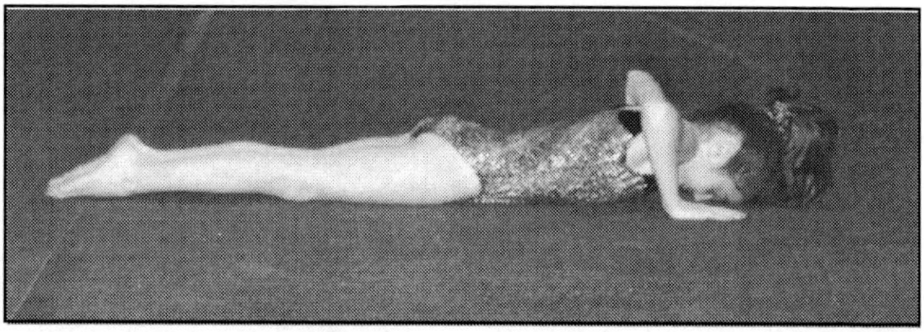

Common Mistakes:

1. not establishing a tripod base with head and hands while dragging legs forward
2. bending knees while lifting legs
3. not arching back, resulting in legs not being straight up (back is bent with rear end out)
4. allowing arms to wobble or collapse

Tip-Up (2-point balance on hands)

Teaching Tips:

1. start on mat from a squat position
2. place hands on mat shoulder width apart with fingers wide apart
3. bend elbows and rest knees on elbows
4. lean forward while raising head in a "bull-neck" position
5. look a yard to two forward to maintain "bull-neck"
6. maintain 2-point balance with hands on mat and knees resting on elbows for 5 seconds

Common Mistakes:

1. placing hands too close together and with fingers together
2. looking down instead of forward, resulting in head dropping to mat into a tripod

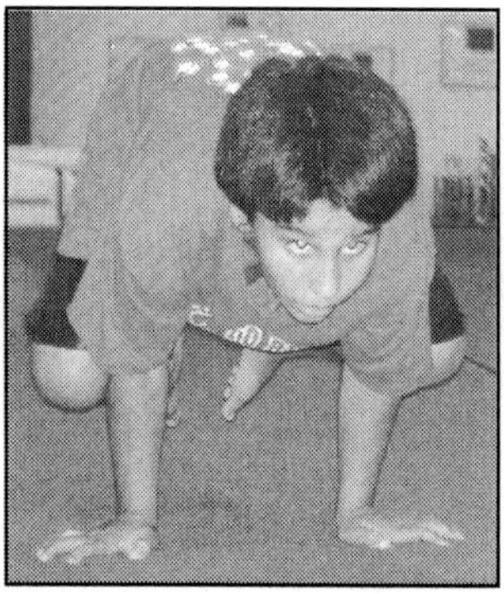

Handstand

Teaching Tips:

1. place hands out in front a little wider than shoulder width apart (suggest pointing fingers forwardA)
2. bend your neck slightly ("bull-neck" and look forward a few feet to keep your neck bent and your back slightly arched
3. with arms straight and locked at the elbows, kick legs up behind you, keeping back slightly arched and looking forward
4. a spotter is needed to stop legs from going over, perhaps to lift legs up so arms are straight and locked,

and to assist as needed in establishing balance; spotter can also guide or hold at the waist to help establish balance

5. concentrate on arching back slightly and keeping legs straight and knees and feet together
6. point toes and stretch legs toward the ceiling
7. hold steady for a 3 to 5-count
8. beginners should come down the same way they went up, lowering legs to the mat; later after they learn the forward roll, they can learn to tuck their chin, bend their arms, lower their body and roll out of the hand stand

Hand stand can also be learned against a wall

Teaching Tips:

1. hands placed on mat slightly in front, shoulder width apart (fingers pointing forward)
2. important to look forward ("bull-neck"), so that if you collapse you will not come down on the back of your neck
3. keeping arms straight and locked and maintaining a "bull-neck" while continually looking slightly forward, kick up so that heels rest against the wall
4. very slightly/softly push off wall with heals (about 3 inches or so), with heels softly bouncing back and forth against the wall while trying to establish balance

5. come down same way you went up, maintaining a "bull-neck" and always looking slightly forward
6. need a spotter to assist in case arms collapse, and perhaps to help lift legs and place them against the wall; also to immediately lift legs up if arms bend, especially if no "bull-neck" to prevent performer from coming down on the back of neck which could result in serious injury

Common Mistakes:

1. not keeping arms straight and locked
2. not "bull-necking" and looking forward
3. not arching back slightly
4. not keeping legs straight (knees are bent) and together
5. allowing arms to bend, wobble or collapse
6. practicing without a spotter!

Log Roll

Teaching Tips:

1. student lies on belly and then moving from belly to back to belly simply rolls down the mat with a straight body
2. arms are either overhead or tucked at the chest
3. important to keep students well spaced so they do not roll on top of each other

Common Mistake:

1. student rolls to the side off the mat instead of rolling straight

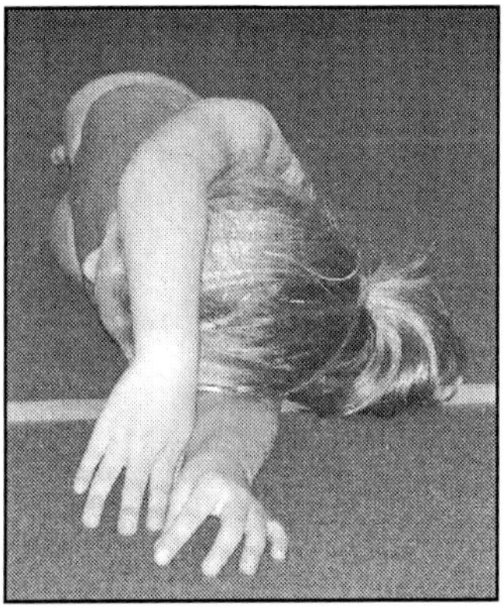
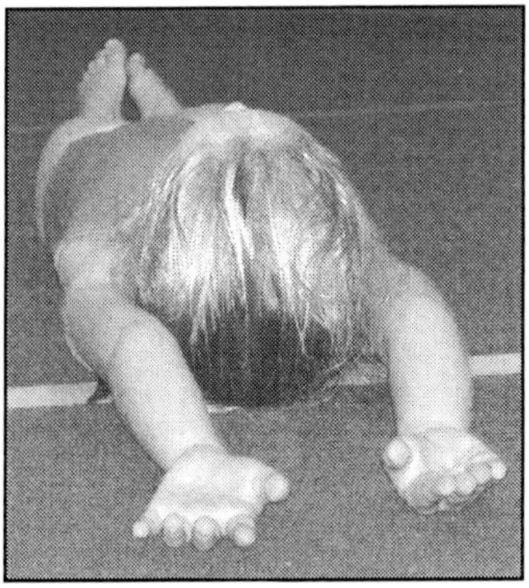

Shoulder Roll

Teaching Tips:

1. start from a squat position on the mat with knees together
2. tuck head to right and into chest
3. bring left shoulder and arm across and into the chest
4. bend and roll over left shoulder and back, finishing in a squat position on toes

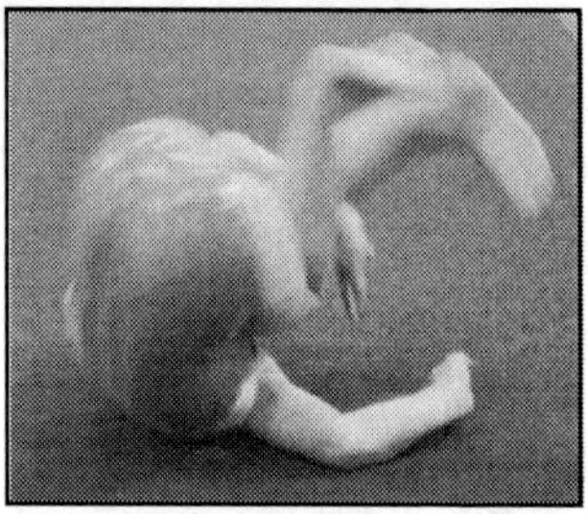

Common Mistake:

1. leaning or rolling only to the side (instead of back too), resulting in tipping to the side instead of completing the roll

Forward Roll

Teaching Tips:

1. start from a squat position on mat with knees together
2. hands flat on the mat, shoulder width apart, fingers pointing forward
3 bend head into the chest
4. push off the balls of feet
5. keeping head tucked, roll over the round of your back (not head or neck)
6. grabbing ankles as you roll will keep you in a ball, speed up roll and pull you to your feet in a squat position
7. finish roll on feet in a squat position
8. place hands in front, head in chest, push off and continue with another forward roll

Common Mistakes:

1. head not in chest; therefore back not bent enough
2. left or right hand collapsing, resulting in a lean, tip or collapse to the side
3. not keeping tucked in a ball
4. not rolling fast enough to make it through the entire roll and finish on toes

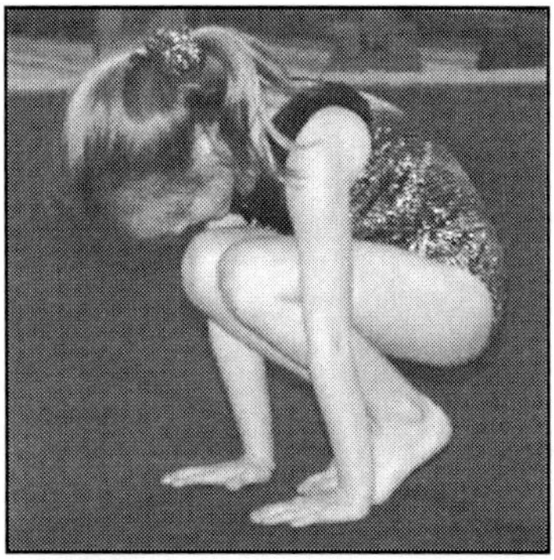

Dive Forward Roll

(similar to forward roll; *but do not attempt unless forward roll is mastered)*

Teaching Tips:

1. start from a squat or semi-squat position
2. push off from squat and spring forward a short distance
3. break fall/dive with hands
4. tuck chin in chest, roll over round of back
5. continue with good forward roll form
6. grab ankles and pull yourself back to a squat position on toes
7. push off and spring forward into another dive roll
8. gradually increase distance of dive if form is good and when comfortable doing so
9. if form is good and when comfortable, can begin dive roll from standing position with feet together, knees bent, and hands overhead instead of from a squat position; follow through with good forward roll form
10. can practice diving over a rolled up mat, but first walk up to mat, reach over mat and place hands on other side of mat, then push off with feet, bending back with chin in chest and following with good forward roll form

Common Mistakes:

1. not getting any distance at all with the "dive"
2. not following through with good forward roll form (could result in injury)

Forward Straddle Roll

Teaching Tips:

1. begin with legs straight and apart in a straddle or V-position
2. place hands close together in between legs
3. bend head into chest and look between legs to get momentum going forward
4. roll over round of back, keeping legs straight and in a V-position throughout the entire roll
5. coming out of roll again place hands in front, close together and in between legs
6. lift seat off the mat with hands and keep back bent by looking in between legs to continue forward momentum in order to go into another straddle roll

Common Mistakes:

1. not keeping legs straight and apart throughout the roll
2. not placing hands in front to lift seat off the mat
3. not bending back and looking between legs to continue forward momentum
4. straightening or looking up instead of keeping back bent, resulting in dropping back on seat

Backward Roll

Teaching Tips:

1. from a squat position with knees together, bend elbows with hands shoulder width apart with palms facing up and fingers pointing backward
2. tuck chin in chest and roll backward over seat and round of back

3. roll over palms of both hands which remain shoulder width apart near ears
4. keep chin tucked in chest and land lightly on toes in a squat position
5. keep chin tucked, reach back with palms of hands, push off and roll over seat, round of back and palms into another backward roll
6. spot by standing to the side of tumbler and lifting up on hips with both hands as the tumbler rolls

Common Mistakes:

1. opening up instead of keeping chin in chest
2. collapsing one hand or shoulder instead of rolling over palms of both hands, resulting in tipping to the side of collapsed hand or shoulder
3. landing on knees instead of toes in a squat position

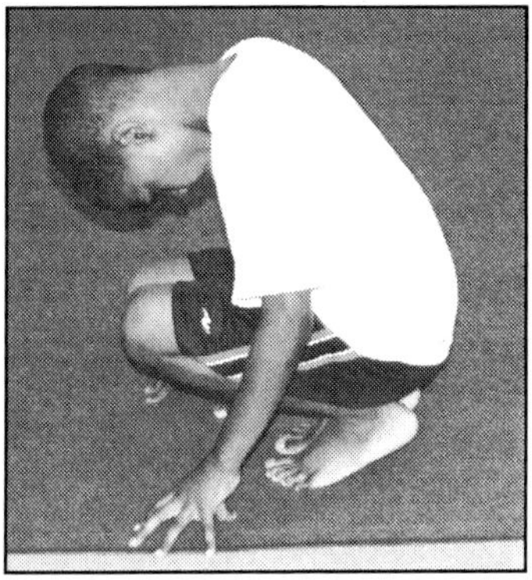

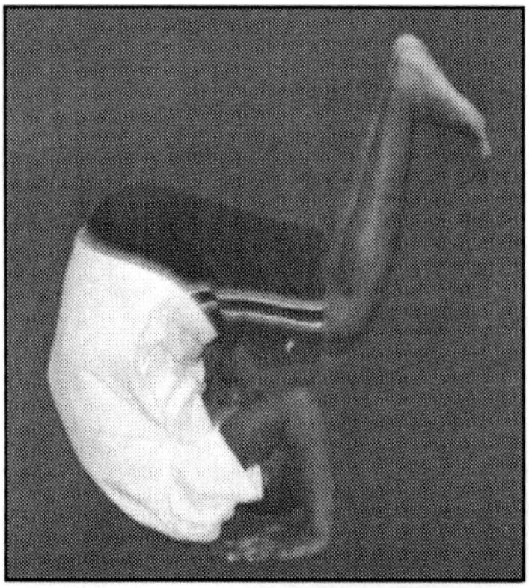

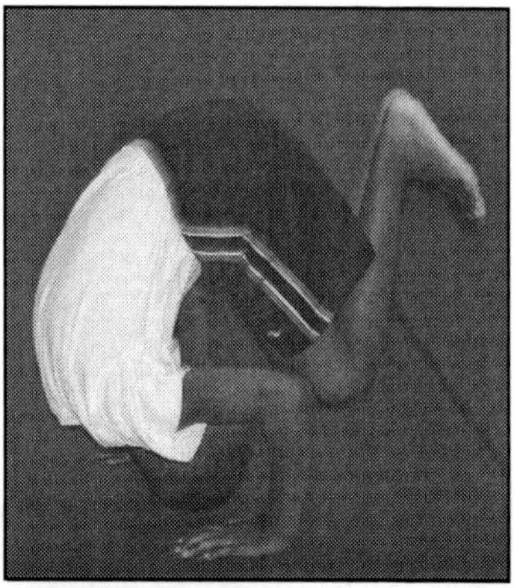

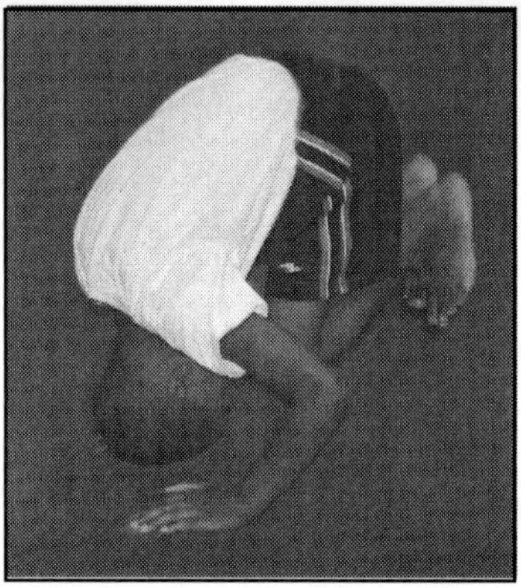

Backward Straddle Roll

Teaching Tips:

1. from a squat position with legs straight and apart in a straddle or V-position and hands between the legs (can start from a regular backward roll position and during backward roll straighten legs to side in a straddle position)

2. tuck chin into chest and roll backward
3. roll over seat and round of back
4. reach back and roll over palms of both hands
5. keep legs straight and apart throughout entire roll
6. repeat to continue with another backward straddle roll
7. if successful, can then begin rolling back from a standing straddle position
8. spot by standing behind the tumbler to lift up the hips; if tumbler is doing a series of rolls, spotter walks backward down the mat ahead of the tumbler

Common Mistakes:

1. bending legs
2. legs are not far enough apart in V-position

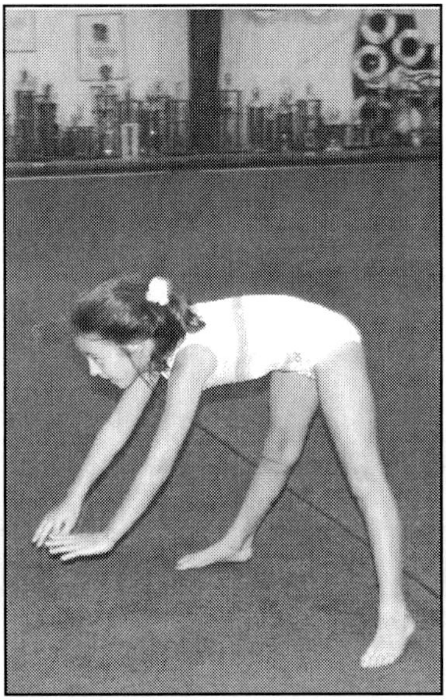

Backward Roll Extension

Teaching Tips:

1. do a backward roll to the point of placing palms flat on the mat a little bit wider than shoulder width apart
2. use momentum of roll while simultaneously pushing up with hands, extending arms and locking elbows, and thrusting legs toward the ceiling
3. arms are straight and locked in a hand stand position
4. legs are straight and together with toes pointed in a momentary handstand
5. snap down into a standing position with both feet landing together (see below as it is similar to landing in a

round-off); or could lower one leg at a time and backward walk out of the extension

Common Mistakes:

1. bending arms in handstand instead of locking elbows to keep arms straight
2. thrusting legs too soon or too late
3. not arching back so handstand is straight up (rear end sticking out)

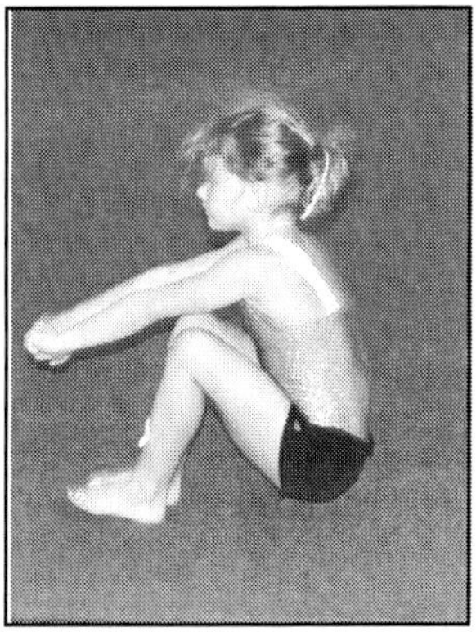

Backward Extension to Chest Roll

Teaching Tips:

1. go into a backward extension
2. at the top of the extension while in a momentary handstand
3. bend elbows, arch back and slowly lower yourself to the mat, scooping or rolling off the chest and thighs
4. when rolling off chest and thighs the toes never hit the mat

Common Mistakes:

1. not going into a full handstand before lowering into the chest roll
2. not arching the back so that the chest comes into contact with the mat first

Cartwheel

Teaching Tips:

1. determine if you are going to do a left-left cartwheel or a right-right cartwheel
2. if left-left, start from a standing position with arms overhead and hands open
3. step forward with left foot (left knee bent)
4. turn body to the left, bend over and place left hand on the mat, with fingers pointing left (hand placement in line with foot), followed by right hand; (hand placement can be learned by first standing to the right of a line on the floor and bending and placing hands on the line to the left)
5. swing right leg upward, keeping legs straight and apart (split or V position)
6. as right leg swings upward, place right hand on mat with fingers pointing left, about shoulder width apart and in line with left hand already on mat pointing left
7. with both hands now on mat and arms straight and locked at the elbow, both legs should swing up toward the ceiling.
8. 8. concentrate on keeping legs straight and apart in a split or V position
9. slightly arch back so that legs will be up straight and not angled to the side
10. left leg lands first, followed by right leg
11. if right-right, then step forward with right foot and place right hand to the right side with fingers pointing right; everything else also opposite of left-left; (hand placement can first be learned by standing to the left of

a line on the floor and bending and placing hands on the line at the right)

Common Mistakes:

1. mixing up the step with left foot/hands pointing left, with step with the right foot/ hands pointing right (it's either left left, or right right)
2. placing hands on mat at same time instead of one and then the other
3. placing hands in front with fingers pointing forward instead of to the side
4. bending the elbows so that the arms are not straight
5. not keeping legs straight and apart throughout cartwheel
6. not arching back so that the cartwheel is not straight up but tilted

Round-Off

Teaching Tips:

1. start out the same as a cartwheel
2. at the top of the cartwheel, rotate hips, bend back and turn in direction that you came from
3. snap legs down and land with both feet at the same time and with feet together

Common Mistakes:

1. not going to the top of the cartwheel before rotating hips (results in "jumping through the move")
2. not landing with legs and feet together
3. not snapping the legs down and landing with feet together and at same time

Tinsica (Cartwheel with a quarter turn)

Teaching Tips:

1. start out with a cartwheel
2. at top of cartwheel, arch back and rotate hips so that you are now facing forward in the direction that you were going
3. land with feet together or step out one foot before the other

Common Mistakes

1. not going to the top of the cartwheel
2. failing to rotate hips in the direction you are going (opposite of round-off)
3. failure to arch back (opposite of round-off)

Kip

Teaching Tips:

1. lay flat on your back
2. roll back on shoulders, placing palms of hands on mat near ears with fingers pointing back, while simultaneously bending back bringing legs over top of chest so that toes are above or behind head
3. keep legs together and straight

4. simultaneously push hard off mat with hands while arching back and snapping legs forward, upward and outward at about a 45 degree angle
5. spring to feet with soles of feet in tight close to buttocks, landing in standing position with knees bent

Common Mistakes:

1. failure to thrust legs forward at the correct angle
2. failure to push forcefully off mat with hands
3. failure to arch back

Headspring

Teaching Tips:

1. place a folded mat or two or rolled up mat across width of another mat
2. have spotters sit or kneel on one knee on each end of rolled up or folded mat so mat will not move; also to spot, and if needed, assist tumbler arch back by placing a hand in the small of the back
3. tumbler steps toward mat and simultaneously places head and hands on mat shoulder width apart
4. start as if doing a forward roll off mat but midway through roll forcefully push off mat with hands similar to doing a kip
5. also, like a kip, arch back and thrust legs forward, upward and outward at a 45 degree angle and land on feet with knees bent
6. basically a forward roll that midway through turns into a kip (kip out of roll)
7. midway through the move the people kneeling on sides of mat can place their outside hands in middle of tumbler's back to force an arch if an arch is not there
8. need another spotter standing on the mat in front where the tumbler will complete the move to break the tumbler's momentum and prevent the tumbler from falling forward

Common Mistakes:

1. failure to push off mat with hands
2. failure of tumbler to thrust legs at the proper angle
3. failure to arch back (result will be a forward roll or tumbler landing on back)
4. failure of teacher to use spotters as well as to teach where spotters should be, what to look for and how to spot

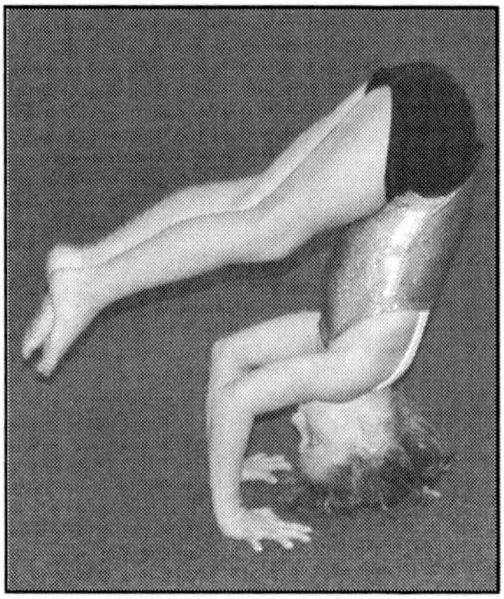

Handspring

(similar to head spring except head is not placed on mat)

Teaching Tips:

1. need same spotters doing the same thing as for headspring
2. tumbler steps toward mat and places hands on mat shoulder width apart
3. arms remain straight
4. push forcefully off mat with arms while simultaneously arching back and thrusting legs forward, upward and outward at a 45 degree angle
5. tumblers lands on feet with knees slightly bent
6. spotter needs to be out in front to break tumbler's momentum in case the tumbler starts to fall forward

Common Mistakes:

1. failure to fully extend arms
2. failure to arch back so as to land on feet
3. failure to have spotters and teach how to spot

Chapter 3

EXAMPLES OF TUMBLING COMBINATIONS

Depending upon the skill level of individuals, students who can do several skills can try to string together various combinations of skills. *As always, remember that these are students and not members of a gymnastics team.* Some examples of combinations could be:

1. Forward roll, step into a cartwheel, round-off, backward straddle roll into a backward extension into a chest roll.
2. Forward roll, tip-up, tri-pod, headstand, forward roll out of headstand, rock back and kip out into a dive roll, step into a round-off
3. Head stand from a prone position, forward roll out, step into a tinsica, dive roll, step into a round-off, backward roll into an extension into a chest roll.
4. Front scale into a Swedish Fall, pull into a headstand, forward roll out, step into a cartwheel, round-off, backward roll, tip-up, tri-pod, headstand.

Chapter 4

EXAMPLES OF BASIC PARTNER ACTIVITIES AND GROUP STUNTS

Angle Stand

Teaching Tips:

1. partner B stands in front of partner A, with back to A
2. partner A bends knees so partner B can step on partner A's thighs
3. partner A holds partner B by the waist while partner B steps up
4. partner A grabs partner B above the knees
5. partner A leans back while holding partner B around the thighs
6. partner B arches back and leans forward with arms stretched to the sides
7. should have a spotter standing in front in case partner B falls forward

Common Mistakes:

1. partner A does not have or maintain a firm grip on partner B's thighs
2. partner A does not lean back to establish balance

3. partner B does not arch back and therefore falls forward
4. failure to use and properly place spotters

Chest Stand

Teaching Tips:

1. partner A is on hands and knees
2. partner B stands to the side and places chest on partner A's back
3. partner B reaches underneath and raps arms around partner A's stomach
4. partner B one leg at a time lifts or kicks straight up and arches back
5. partner B maintains chest stand for 5 seconds
6. a spotter can assist partner B lift legs

Common Mistakes:

1. partner A cannot maintain a stable bottom position and collapses
2. partner B cannot kick up into a chest stand or hold a chest stand

Knee Shoulder Stand

Teaching Tips:

1. partner A lays on back on mat with knees bent, feet close to seat and arms straight and up and angled across chest
2. partner B stands in front of A's feet and places hands on A's knees
3. partner B leans across partner A with B resting shoulders into A's hands
4. partner B then kicks up into shoulder stand with A pulling B slightly forward
5. partner A and B both maintain straight arms with elbows locked
6. partner B keeps head forward by looking into partner A's eyes

7. partner B maintains shoulder stand for 5 seconds
8. should have spotters on side and front in case partner B has trouble getting into shoulder stand or falls from shoulder stand; also if need be to help B into shoulder stand

Common Mistakes:

1. one or both partners do not maintain straight arms with locked elbows
2. partner B does not maintain grip on partner A's knees
3. partner B cannot kick up into shoulder stand and/or hold shoulder stand position
4. partner A bends arms or cannot hold partner B stable
5. partner B does not look at A's eyes, therefore does not maintain arched back
6. failure to use or properly position spotters

Swan Balance

Teaching Tips:

1. partner A lays on back with knees slightly bent
2. partner B stands facing partner A
3. partner A places soles of feet on B's hips and upper thighs with feet pointing to side
4. partner B leans into A's feet while simultaneously holding B's hands
5. partner A with legs straight lifts up and with feet pulls B across chest
6. partner B lifts head and feet and arches back and, when balanced, lets go of A's hands
7. partner B hold swam balance for 3 to 5 seconds
8. should have spotters on both sides in case B loses balance or falls

Common Mistakes:

1. partner A does not keep legs straight or lift B across body
2. partner B cannot lift head and does not arch back to establish balance
3. partner A cannot establish or hold a steady bottom position
4. failure to use or properly position spotters

3-2-1 Pyramid

Teaching Tips:

1. explain directions and establish position of people before building the pyramid
2. three largest people in group on hands and knees facing instructor
3. two next largest people standing behind them facing instructor
4. smallest person in group standing behind the two people facing instructor
5. when instructed, middle two people place their hands and knees on top of bottom three, each with their inside hand and knee on middle person in bottom row and outside hand and knee on end person on their side in bottom row
6. with assistance the smallest person climbs on top of middle two, placing one hand and one knee on back of each person in middle row
7. all people in pyramid look at instructor
8. when instructor says 'break,' outside people in bottom and middle rows quickly roll to their outside, with middle person on bottom quickly rolling either right or left, allowing top person to drop onto the mat
9. all people need to keep arms in so as no one will fall on extended arms

Common Mistakes:

1. people climb on backs of people before receiving directions
2. outside people in bottom two rows do not roll fast enough, resulting in top person landing on top of someone

Monkey Roll (Figure 8 pattern)

Teaching Tips:

1. three people of similar size-A, B and C- lie on their bellies about two feet a part facing the instructor
2. instructor explains directions
3. middle person (B) rolls to the left toward C
4. C dives over B and rolls on belly-to- back-to belly toward A
5. A now dives over C and rolls on belly-to- back-to-belly toward B
6. B dives over A and rolls toward C
7. C dives over B and rolls toward A
8. Continue with the figure-8 pattern of inside person always rolling and outside people always diving and rolling toward the middle

Common Mistakes:

1. people dive on their belly and just lay there clogging up the middle, instead of diving and rolling, diving and rolling
2. one or more people move too slowly, causing the action to stop
3. instead of always facing the same direction, someone may turn and face the opposite direction
4. person in the middle may try to dive to the outside instead of rolling to the outside
5. people on the outside may try to roll toward the middle instead of diving toward the middle

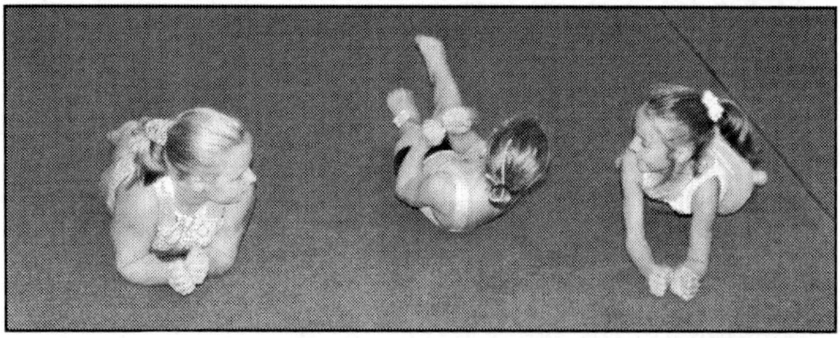

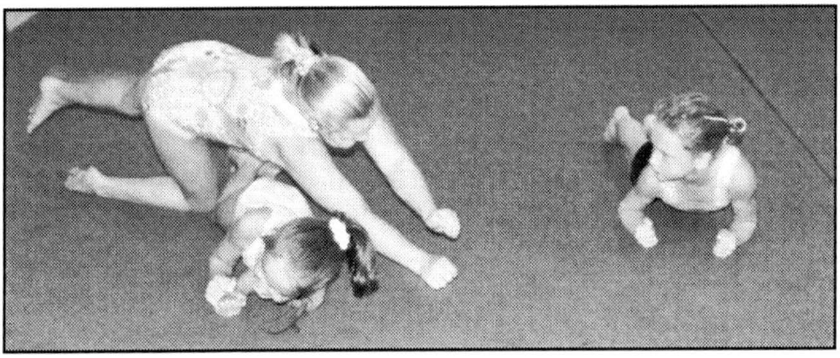

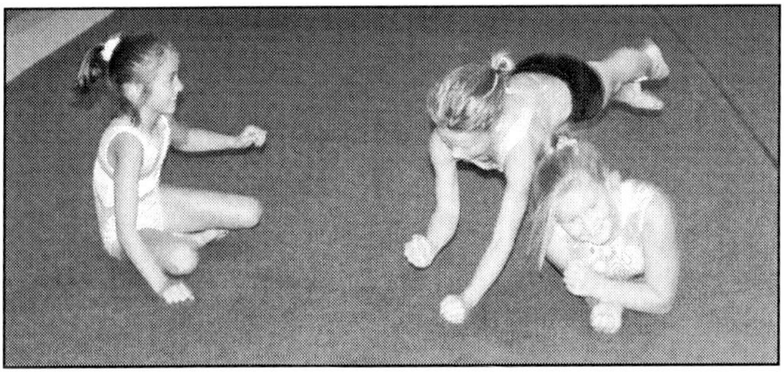

Chain/Partner Forward Roll

Teaching Tips:

1. partner A lies on back with head facing near end of mat with legs lifted into the air and slightly a part
2. partner B stands behind partner A's head and using the hands and thumbs firmly grabs partner A's ankles
3. partner A reaches back and with hands and thumb firmly grabs partner B's ankles
4. partner B leans forward and with head bent, neck tucked into chest and back rounded, pushes off to begin forward roll
5. partner A lifts partner B's ankles and guides B forward while simultaneously lifting upper body to begin forward roll
6. coming around partner B now lifts A's ankles and guides A into forward roll
7. continue down the mat doing a partner or chain forward roll
8. chain roll need not be fast but can be done slowly, so long as both partners maintain grip on each other's ankles and assist each other by helping lift partner into the next roll

Common Mistakes:

1. one or both partners let go of ankles (if so, maneuver breaks down)
2. either partner does not round back to establish proper forward roll form and to maintain momentum needed for continuing chain roll

Elephant Walk

Teaching Tips:

1. students A and B face each other
2. B puts arms around A's neck and jumps up and locks legs at ankles around A's waist
3. B bends backward and walks on hands between A's legs while keeping legs locked at the ankles around A's waist
4. A bends over and puts hands on mat
5. A walks forward with B hanging on

Common Mistake:

1. B does not keep ankles locked

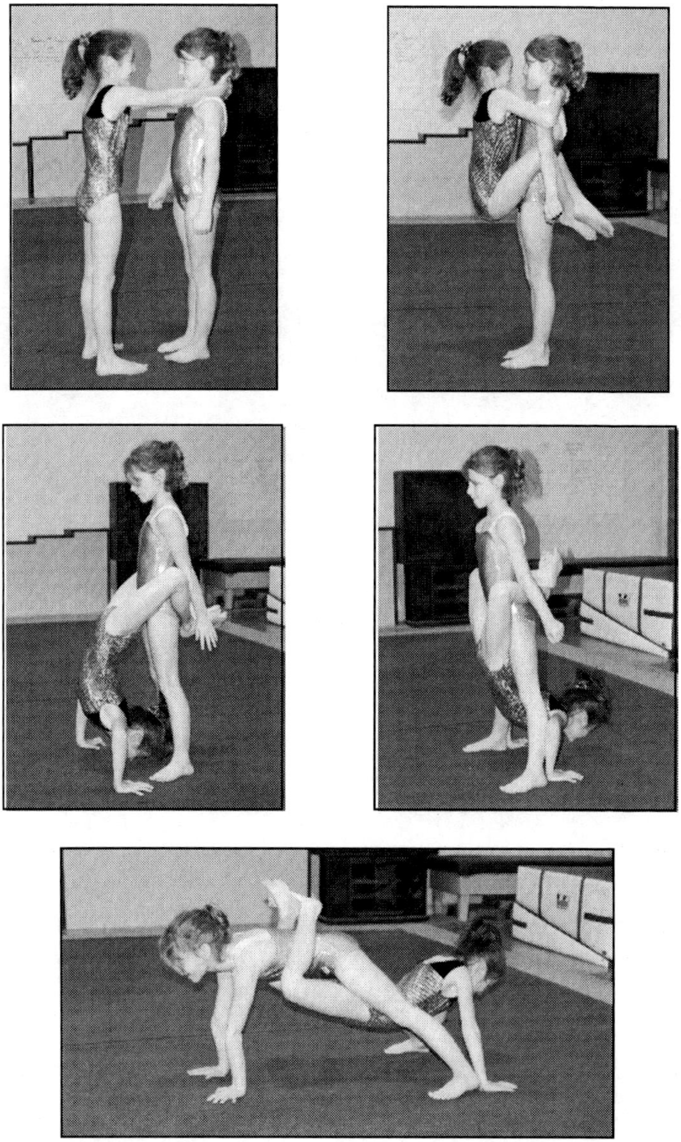